Here Not There

Here Not There

Edited by
Judith Beveridge & Carolyn Rickett

Puncher & Wattmann

First published in 2012

Published by Puncher and Wattmann
PO Box 441
Glebe NSW 2037

http://www.puncherandwattmann.com

puncherandwattmann@bigpond.com

National Library of Australia
Cataloguing-in-Publication entry:

Here Not There
ISBN 9781921450754

I. Title.

A821.3

Cover design by Kayla Wolf, 'That Design' Intern

Printed by McPhersons Printing Group

For Robyn Priestley

Dedicating a volume of poetry to an historian may seem odd—until you know Robyn Priestley. Robyn's interests in the Arts are broad and her love of and respect for creativity is great. Just talking to her quickly reveals a mind full of curiosity, a sense of wonder, and a delight in language, which surely are the foundations of a poetic soul. Her personal interest in great literature has been reflected in her reading and her outings to many significant theatre and cultural events. If there was a creative performance of any kind at Avondale, you could count on Robyn's active support. At art exhibitions, poetry readings, musical concerts, book launches, there was Robyn cheering you on for your accomplishments.

Robyn also has a long history at Avondale. A total of 36 years, the last 30 of them continuous, represents a huge investment of talent, vision and commitment to the Arts at Avondale. In her former role as Dean of the Faculty of Arts and current position as Head of the School of Humanities and Creative Arts, she has shown a keen interest in the work of the literati, and constantly encouraging initiative and creativity in Communication and English studies.

It is a pleasure for your students and colleagues to dedicate this volume of poetry to you, Robyn, for you have so often supported us. This is your moment in the sun in thanks for your rich contribution to the creative endeavours of Arts at Avondale.

—Associate Professor Daniel Reynaud
Dean of Faculty of Arts and Theology

Contents

Introduction

In her recent memoir entitled *Reading by Moonlight: How Books Saved a Life*, Brenda Walker highlights the ways in which reading and writing literature can sustain a person during times of deep crisis. One of the literary texts Walker repeatedly refers to as having this kind of positive effect on her is Samuel Beckett's *Malone Dies.* She writes: "I never tire of reading it; it steadies me, as Dante may have steadied Beckett, as Tennyson's sunset and evening star may have steadied my grandmother." While such a book title might ironically evoke a grim and foreboding prospect, Walker suggests there is something simultaneously empowering about Beckett's protagonist who, armed with a pencil and exercise book, continues to write through and beyond his confined circumstances.

This notion of writing (and by logical extension reading) as a means of expansion is so beautifully realised in Malone's mantra of "Live and invent." These two verbs signify the shaping imagination and applied action of artists who want to make an impact upon their readers. The idea of drawing on life experiences and the imagination to invent something new for a reader informs the poetry selected for this anthology; always at work is a desire to bring the reader into the distilled moment of being present.The poems in this anthology will undoubtedly produce a range of effects; some poems may delight, while others seek to confront; there are acts of mourning, occasions of celebration; instances of play and sombre reveries; homage sits beside satirical critique; stillness quickly gives way to the frenetic; and remembering tries, as always, to stop forgetfulness. These poets, a collaboration of first-time poets along with those whose craft has been honed through experience, have invented familiar and unfamiliar worlds for the reader to enter (or re-enter) with them.

And by way of editorial invitation to enter these diverse poetic spaces, we begin with Vera Newsom's poem "Gratia" as both a tribute and prelude:

Now that the wind has dropped
You can walk in the garden.

It doesn't matter if
a small rain falls. Buds

will open wide, trees
lift higher;

in the quiet light
new work prosper.

—Judith Beveridge and
Carolyn Rickett

Works Cited

Beckett, Samuel. *Malloy, Malone Dies, The Unnamable*. New York: Alfred A. Knopf, 1997, p 20.

Newsom, Vera. *Gratia: New and Selected Poems*. Melbourne: Five Islands Press Pty Ltd, 2007, p 213.

Walker, Brenda. *Reading by Moonlight: How Books Saved a Life*. Australia: Penguin Group, 2010, p 17.

These words (this gift, this poem).

—Rosemary Dobson, "The Anthropologist".

Japanese Cranes

Their frames—
an architecture of paper,
lightweight beams.

A low sun
huddles into fir trees, ponds—
trims the landscape.

Only the small,
or poised, will survive:
these birds'

light breakable beauty.
Mating—they are
the original origami:

one unritualised peck
could chip them.
Such a skilled brittle

elegance. Earth can crack
its icy ceramic:
so their dance is brief,

a perfect choreography.
Their cries—
the rattle of tea-sets

kept intact
by ceremony.
And when they lift—

they could be glass
blown from a white
clear flame.

JUDITH BEVERIDGE

Herons at Dusk

This is the time of day when the light runs down the sky
like bluing and meets the bay, when whipbirds set acoustic
flares along the trees, when I'll stand and listen to the yachts,
a sound as if cutlery were being replenished on tabletops;

but most of all when I love to watch the herons step along
the shore, how like tai chi performers they will step deftly,
easily into constantly reconfigured stances. I can see one
down by the mangroves now, moving and then redoing

each step as though it has become fastidious about how
to present the curve of is neck, a punctilio it must get right
before it will allow itself to stand twinned to its reflection.
Near the pier another heron is holding its bill over the reeds

as purposeful as a seiner with a marlinespike, before it
jabs then returns to its wire-drawn stance, as if all it must
achieve now is to lift and pull itself into the distance
like sail twine. When the herons quietly step they make

even the stilts' and avocets' neat stabs along the sand
seem like slapstick; they make the routines of all who fish
along the shore at dusk seem over-weighted and vaudevillian.
And look! how they stand—at last—stilled to perfection.

Life Lived Towards

(after the painting "Chichester Canal" by J. M.W. Turner)

Among the mists,
beyond the pull of time,
where silent ghosts of ships
in blue dawn wait for burning sun,

our lives gleam swiftly, and are gone.

We wait, misplaced in morning's peace,
hungry for flash of rising day.
The water staring back at us
inquires:

how have our hearts fared
these last tumultuous years? Have we so listened
that we now can hear
the whispers of those loves long gone

and echoes of infinity that sound
as tide drifts out forever to the sea?

Let us answer:

we live here
towards there
looking straight ahead
to dawn,

and when the sun at last
peals forth in glory,
what will the morning hold
on that last day?

KIMCHENG BOEY

Chinatowns

for Andrew Pritchard

Each an outpost, a piece of China
forever China, a bit of the Middle
Kingdom transplanted, grafted
on the white devils' soil, earthed now
to a different dragon spirit. Where do we go to
but one of these embassies of the body
when the spirit's hunger clashes its cymbals
and beats its dragon drum?

Pai Fang

Kinship, memory, regret, a heady mix quickening as you
pass under the gate-arch, the gold-embossed calligraphy
"Four Seas As Home" ushering in a remote part of you, the flanking
lions guardians to a world that mirrors the dream
of home. And the dialects all add up to a language you have lost,
the names of shops and restaurants, the parade of souvenir
and grocery stores, the familiar-strange faces, the sounds
of these far-flung provinces a password into a China of the self.

Tang Ren Jie

Street of the Tang people, where we can pretend
to be Chinese again, can quote Li Bai and Du Fu in a strange accent
that half-rhymes with something lost and part-rhymes
with translated voices caught from living a different dream,
as if we have never left, never been transplanted,
only pickled in a alien tongue, the sounds of the words
like souls separated from their body, their characters like ghosts
wavering, tethering us to this neither here-nor-there world.

Emperor's Garden, Sydney

Carts of stacked bamboo steamers navigating
the noisy tables; in a different Chinatown
you knew this as dim sum, point heart,
the ha gao you loved picked out and thong-transferred
to the lazy susan you spun like a roulette wheel.
The other tables were festive with families, the steamers
emptying fast; at your table only Mum and Sis, Father's
absence hovering like ghostly steam over the waiting dishes.

Melbourne

The shellacked duck, the glistening braids
of roast pork, these fowls, these meats, the cleaver
and the man behind the altar-like chopping block, denizens
of Chinatowns elsewhere, a common language
of a menu that devours you and awakens tastebuds
untranslated, the braised phoenix claws and duck wings,
the stewed giblets, all framed in the window;
a tableau that composes you as you devour it.

Sussex Street, Sydney

The wizened old man in Mao cap scratching out mournful notes
on his *er hu*, the sounds at first slack, then growing into a recognisable
tune, as though a lost map is being reassembled, the demolished
hutong in Beijing or the old quarter in Shanghai. In high school I learned
to drag the horse-hair bow across and between the two strings, homesick sobs
I couldn't understand, forgotten till now, as the long cadenzas
of grief seize and ply me between the chords of the lost
and the dead, pentatonic measures between memory and home.

PETER BOYLE

Towns in the great desert (11)

What mattered most in the dream
was the quality of blue in the water
so that it wasn't about the naked young man, my rival,
doing handstands and backflips into the canal
or any wince of pain from contemplating in reverse image
the hammered remnants of my own body.
Like the perfect alignment of sailboats on a blue sea,
between the world and the world
the canal made a corridor
for whales and the white refuse of icebergs
to drift between familiar department stores,
the takeaway, the news-stand and the corner pub.
Suddenly how far away from death I was
standing alone and speechless
before the waters of the sky,
this proof
that the depths go on shining.

Nightpoems
18/1/2012

The banker who owns the stars took me to his observatory on a hill outside Rome. "Look," he said, "that one is where I will live and that one is for my daughter and that one where my wife will live." "Do people who have no money also go to stars after they die?" I ask. "Of course," he shrugs calmly, "they will have to spend their time with the worms but nothing stops a federation of them owning a share in a star. The worms too have their shimmering presence laced in the stillness above and, besides, who can say how many emperors' stars have followed the laws of combustion, dwindling away in the cavalcade of what we can only call the wounds in brightness." "Will the sky and the stars end?" I ask him. He is silent and pulls from his pocket a heavy golden watch within which can be seen smaller golden watches each containing more watches and the last, the smallest, specks of gold sand. The banker is a sober citizen who regulates the profit and loss of the journey. His immense computations are held in a wooden drawer where wands of mercury assess their truth. Now on his outstretched hand specks of brightness are multiplying and I no longer know what is the sky, what the hand, what the unstated sanctuary of luminous decomposing soil.

JULIAN BREMNER

Middle-Class Maze

Mum stares and so she should,
her boy's grown up.
That safety stair fence has moved,
It changed its name and goes by cul-de-sac now.

No longer a succession plan,
it's a middle class maze.
Dad keeps his job, nine to five.
Mum prattles, where has it gone?
The time that is.

Dad's pattern is less comforting now, more distracting.
No one's died, but something has changed.
Everything is right, but it all feels wrong.
Not kicking out of the nest,
but jumping.
One's coming of age is another's going.

That circle of life is more a line.
It grows from green to green, with a grey middle.
Coffee cup sentiment tells her that is was the grey parts,
the undefined ones that were the best.
No comfort, when all there is, is green.
It's the in-between they want, hers and his, their greatest work is in him.
And it seems its finished, time to find something else.

Not so fast the son says,
I am not some bourgeois experiment.
I still need preening,
the gardener didn't show—
even this tired metaphor could use a trim.

And so we grow up and we change,
often a casualty of choice, a dilution.
One part wisdom,
six parts indecision.
And it's taking longer to get there,
in this middle-class maze.

JULIAN BREMNER

This God, Me

I stand atop my own Mount Olympus;
receiving not Zeus, Ares or Jesus.
My power is mine own;
Zeus your lightning has lost its spark.
So salutations and celebrations,
Bacchus write the invites.

Tink Tink Tink,
I'm hammering.
Chip Chip Chip,
It's good to be king.

Sculpting, forming my own deity.
Machiavelli, it is I pulling your strings.
Rising a pillar of cloud no less,
the swelling crowds clamour to catch a glimpse.
Praise be to Allah, not today.

Clink Clink Clink,
I'm banking.
Bow Bow Bow,
Now praise me.

You've reached your end,
thunderclap mortality.
No shadow, it's spring.
Mt. Olympus is a hill,
And no gods remain.

Roses for Crianlarich

These roses are not crushed or repentant.
Blood-scarlet, the petals sculpt time. Moments
slip by, a clock ticks, the refrigerator drones
and the iced-rain loosens in slow drips to earth.

Do they ask me to punctuate or unburden,
neither, or both in what measure? I am uncertain.
There is a road from Tarbet to Crianlarich, a low
pass to chase and patience are what one needs.

Keep your eyes wide for dark clouds stretch out,
asleep in the heavens, as if they, too, hibernate.
Shut, like oyster bivalves fed to insomniacs,
how we dreamt of morning's pearl. Watch close,

if the road bends or narrows, if your bag is heavy.
Nothing counts but the tramontane wind blowing
from the north. Nothing, but driftwood, are we, so
downy, the little ducks might teach us obedience.

Poor spidery sepals affix the rose petals like arms
crossed for the clutching buds. There is a language
for each knuckle of mountain this sheer light held.
A language tramped this way and was made captive.

MICHELLE CAHILL

Something like a Reverie

It happens that you wake before dawn,
dreaming you walk the empty streets
as unfinished threads of rain stitch their
needlepoints. Your bare feet stumble
over fruit, half-eaten, clipped from trees
where sulphur-crested cockatoos hang,
conspicuous as bleached handkerchiefs.
Their strange cry bids you to wander
after dogs tire of barking or your lover
stirs closer with his inordinate devotion.

You see beyond the drapes of windows
into Federation homes, observe the messy
tangle of arms, to follow the scent of
imagined flowers, their colours masked
by a darkness which is deeper, softer
even, than everything you've buried.
You know the day brings nothing eventful.
Cut lunches, shoelaces, ironed uniforms.
How during school hours the roof creaks,
the lizards escape your tread to and from
the clothesline. How the garden's beauty
defies all reason, being pointless as ever.

Five Love Poems

after Adrienne Rich

I

Heat settles like a blanket
paddled by fan blades
overhead. You left before the sun
came to this place, before
the world stirred. All night,
we were two halves of a clam, opening
and closing in the dark, breathing saltwater.

II

Dusk descends with the screaming
of the birds. They meet in trees
along this avenue. Give them time.
Soon the bats will emerge, silent,
leather wings beating air. If we could tune
our ears to their speech: the moon,
this plum, the steel-white lights.

III

These floorboards, the colour of honey,
were laid end to end by men
with skilled hands. The floor planers laboured
from morning to evening, stopping only
for a mouthful or two of sour
red wine. The cheese crumbled
to salt, tasting of sweat.

IV

Grandmother Pearl knew how to light
a fire. Matches, tinder, charcoal.
A rattan fan splinters over time.
Black tongs place burning coals
into the heart of the iron. It was heavy: harder
to be woman then, but you had days
and days. Oh the children.

V

To give life is alchemy. To take life:
a bucket full of pondwater poured
into the balsam. Music-makers
would write requiems
from the frozen notes of tadpoles.
Now spring will be quiet
and the lilypads, still.

After the Wreck

'Don't shoot me. I am a British object.'
James Morrill, 1863

Drawknives. Spar gauge. Caulking irons
and hollow plane. If I play my cards right,
after this voyage I'll be shipwright. The *Peruvian*,

a beauty of a three-masted barque, cleaves the water
swift. The winds are in our favour this February dawn.
Bound for China with a hold full of coal to trade

for silk and tea. The Captain sets our course for north
and west. For days we skirt the coast, then land recedes
as the southerly blows. One afternoon, without warning,

hard rain that turns into hail – ice large as a man's fist
pounds the deck then shatters. Black clouds roil
as the gale rips into canvas. We fight to lower the sails,

shouting all the while. Rope burns my palms
as rigging snakes upwards. Then the world jars—a great shudder,
an awful splintering of wood— the first mate yells *we are aground*

***

Twenty-two's the magic number. I notch the days
with my solitary knife every sunset. Today, a shark:
we take turns to drink its blood before I cut each man

a palm-sized chunk of flesh. Even the Captain's wife
chews it without compunction. Land teases and withdraws.
We are helpless and adrift. Oh the ocean. This hollow sea.

***

Washed up on this shore. Only five of us left.
The rest in the water, God save their souls. Miller
talks about going for it, for civilisation. All we have:

this canoe, abandoned by natives, its strange markings
long faded by the sun. *Don't go, Miller.* Between us,
carpenter and apprentice, we fashion oars from driftwood.

The Captain blesses the craft. I say nothing
and turn my face away. We push him out
with the tide. Soon he fades into the waves.

***

Miller is gone. The boy White is sick,
fever of a sort that leaves him shivering
at noon but drenched in sweat at night.

We lay him out in a shelter cobbled together
from branches and leaves. The Captain scans the horizon
while I comb the bay for food. His wife has found fruit

and drops them from her skirts onto the sand.
They are so bright against the white grains
I cannot stand to look – a noise from the trees – *men*

* James Morrill was the sole shipwreck survivor from the *Peruvian* to return to white civilisation after seventeen years of living amongst the Bindal people around what was to become the Townsville area.

Poem for My Grandson

> Anon out of the earth a fabric huge
> Rose like an exhalation, with the sound
> Of dulcet symphonies and voices sweet,
> Built like a temple.
>
> — Milton, *Paradise Lost*

I

Dear Archie, out of vows, tonight, out of
sighs and symbols, and the fragile syllables
of heaving speech, a house is being built.
Your mother and my daughter, her lover
and your father, seem preoccupied
with each other, as they should be,
but they are building here a house
of many mansions, and the largest one is yours.
And though this house is built of words and rings
and touches felt and framed as promises,
no words of mine can justly represent it.
We'll have to see it, Archie, for ourselves.

To some, admittedly, a house like theirs
is folly, a delusion by fond *angst* decreed.
To others, it is just a house, no more:
a weathershield of tiles and bricks and mortar.
But in the lineaments of the palpable we trace
a dream as ancient as receding seas.
Just how a house – an empty space that's floored
and walled – becomes a home; how fragments dovetail
into artifice and turn to gather in obliquities
of heart and sunlight, only the heart and sunlight
can explain. I can't. One kitchen prepares food—
another, sacrament. One bedroom offers rest—
another, intimations of a life that finds,
within this life, dim passages to the vital
vexed euphoria we know as charity, or love.

II

Out of vows, then, Archie, comes a house
destined to outlive the signs—the cracks, the shreds—
of temporal decay. Or so I would believe.
And that *behind* the words, behind
the cracks and gaps, behind the wallpaper
curling like dead petals, behind the stains of use,
abuse, and absence lies an occult harmony
and wholeness.
The house your parents conjure up
tonight for you and me, Archie—and for all of those
gathered before and after by their love—
has touched me, for their house *is* touched.
Its silent rooms bespeak the tragi-comedy
of life: content and calm shot through
with frantic care and uncalled suffering;
stages of passion and repose, of anger
and contrition, played without pretending
to more, or less, than all that we can mean.

And at the threshold of this house of many mansions,
Archie, there you are, your father and your mother,
not knowing what stairs and tears, what rooms and dreams
it holds, but ready, now, to take your first giant step.

In a Suburban Graveyard

What, would you die, and so forsake me yet again?
Especially now the shadow of my own grave beckons
from the patchwork twilight? You have abused me
in a thousand ways since that besotted season
when, from your careless but unerring touch,
I learned to follow, and allow.

Just how
could I have known that history was a prison-house
of rituals and redundancies, of roles
inherited from ghosts, though still our own?
I never dared to brook the privilege of your dreams
and disillusionments; fearing your petulance,
I chose to be a stranger in your centred world.

My name is Margaret – common enough, but still
the one I whisper. Did you ever know
the snub-nosed, awkward girl who greyed
and thickened by your side?—ever see or, better,
feel I had a me, and my own dreams?
Or that you had responsibilities
for tenderness, say, for confiding and for hearing
confidences? For holding and beholding? Responsibilities
beyond your semen and your salary?

Of course I'm being bitter, and of course
we had our moments. If I indulge unkindness
the fault is yours. You might at least have stayed
to argue.

In truth, the hunter and the gatherer
was me: hungering after things, and things,
I traded otherness and a thousand lives
for an unremarkable sense of something, well,
familiar, something cribbed and cradled
in the sheet that wound us both in our betrayal.

No, I'm not so sure of flesh as to complain
that you betrayed my body. There were times,
of course; times of sixth sense and nonsense,
times my mind scuttled into fantasy like a crab.
But, no, betrayal was not, is not sexual: a breach
of promises that are more elusive—
like your dying, now, in your careless,
selfish way when you might, just once,
have let me take the lead.

The Manger of Words

In the manger of words
is the bird with its nib in the bark,
is the pitcher's shadow
which contains no water,
are the bells in a field ringing
as if to repeat what life is like.

In the manger of words
stirs language born
from what is slight in the heart—
a fabulous and restless fish,
the bacillus and cliff,
a spider leaping from a broken star.

This language speaks
for the beautiful crane, for the faun
that steps out from the tree,
for the four black crows
flying forever apart.

And as it speaks
the world evolves into silence,
an ever-softening song,
the lasting accompaniment
to all we cannot say.

The Law of Necessity

Is the smallest law.
It's like a street
that has not yet been laid
on a map.
Or dawn
before it's seen
by the trees of the day.
If you follow it
you will eventually come
to the universe
that passes its laws
in a grain of rice.
If you rest there
you will find
that what is needed is sensible
and insane:
in this space the size
of a maggot,
to live, to howl,
to be silent,
to live for as long as death,
all that's possible
is necessary
and most of what exists here
can be comfortably
discarded.
This law is the smallest.
It's like a little spot
on a spot.
Or the grass
whispering ant-things
to your heart.

Air

In my canoe I descend rapidly
down the swollen, muddy river.
My eyes are fixed forward
on the snags ahead.

Without notice, I'm hurled out.
Flung upside down
spun like washing on spin cycle.

Frantically
I fight for air.

Icy water gushes into my lungs.
I splutter
like an asthmatic in need of an inhaler.

I feel my strength fading
as I frantically fight for air.

And then
a hand
with the strength of a thousand oxen
lifts me.

Air—
sweet air.

Falling

Stiff, clammy hands
struggle to grip the greasy rock face.

The old, fraying rope
heaves under her excessive weight.

Silently floundering, she inches upwards.
Sweat rivers down her red face.

The minutes crawl agonisingly by.

Her grip slips.

Like a stone tossed from an elevated bridge
she falls
and is caught—

by the jagged rocks below.

The Sculptures by the Sea

The wind has flipped the day around and left you
Here on the wrong side of both time and light.
For look, the sun is sinking to the sea
And you are still in Sydney.
                                        This must be
How things will come to look (or used to look)
On the day behind the last day: all these swimmers
Dripping into their shadows as they amble
Around and through each other on the sand,
Adhering oozily among the waves
Like ants in honey, speaking in slow motion
Before the unseen cameraman.
                                        Your hand
Is joined to hers on the linen tablecloth
While sunlights dash themselves against the glass
Like seagulls crying to be fed.

The sculptures by the sea are dotted here
And there along the path, the sand, the banks,
The pockmarked rock walls writhing to the north,
A last encrypted lesson: that pack of dogs
Escaping up the rise to the main road,
Their bodies fashioned out of tea-stained leather
As though they'd been fished up with Tollund Man;
That farmyard queue—sheep, geese, a horse, a cow,
A fetching pig—miraculously assembled
In perfectly articulated parts
From farm machines and rusty implements,
In X-ray progress to the shining sea;
The six-foot blade of glass—a slice of wave
Excised from the very surf, implanted and
Made fast against the day.
                                        Look, darling, look.
If you plunged an arm in there you would feel the rip
Dragging you out, back into January,
Your face among the foam and your heart still full.

STEPHEN EDGAR

All Eyes

Look, look, it says, and peels away the night
As it flies on. And there,
A ghostly Ferris wheel frozen in space,
Saturn comes looming at the satellite
With all its shattered rings of icy lace
Exquisitely beyond repair.

So much to see. And now the vast moon, Titan,
Fills the compulsive lens.
Descending through the folds of orange fog,
It peers among the marvels to enlighten
A distant world's attention, all agog
For each new vision that it sends.

Out there, some twenty billion light years hence,
Too far for light to serve,
Who knows what sown and pullulating planet
Has come and gone, an ark of evidence
Interminably circling where it cannot
Be salvaged by the optic nerve?

The fossil in the paginated book
Of shale that once was slime
Falls open and cries, Look. And these sunflowers—
Their yellow is the synonym for Look,
Though they've no word for weary or the hours
The sun has summoned them to climb.

Was it for this the aeons fashioned us?
To look and make it so?
The moth wing's intricately subtle scales,
The fleck of matter in the nucleus
As light as light, your face which never fails
To show me what I cannot know.

"After the lassitudes of blue"

After the lassitudes of blue, the sun: now buttermilk,
now brimful and overflowing, suddenly fierce and red,

about to slip below the chipped and crenellated grime,
but shimmering for this last instant before becoming

those shades of pink that bless and surely must amaze,
dusk an uncertain premise, premonition which cannot last

much longer. The world is swaddled now in undertones,
the rhymes we chant to put an end to doubt,

to all that is mysterious and temptingly unknowable.
To think about a mystery we must imagine it,

maybe as a labyrinth or maze, as forest or lantana stand
but not as nothing or the thing impenetrable,

that would have another tangled name.

*

Something passes by, you turn but nothing's there except,
perhaps, a disturbance in the air, a wobble in the orbit

of a distant world, the glint in an oceanic vent.
Free diving is not entirely free: to go down you leave behind;

and coming back breath is an unremitting currency:
constrained air hammers for release, bubbles rise, burst,

or momentarily make transparent domes
which float the sting beneath. Nothing is defined

in all this visibility. Here matter is miraculous again,
wind a devil's breath, silence a wing in the shuffling air.

Such commingling could be eternity, a beyond beyond all seeing
unravelling heart's battle with time that curves and disappears

in pettifogging words. When day grows dark and unintended
is it better to sense or see? The externality of things, that is enough,

it admits of hidden roots, sap which rises,
bark that strips and burns, the complicated exchange of air,

even the whole tree that falls unnoticed.

*

Impossible to think 'black' or 'blank'. To think any thing
that is not thing: black maw, black hood,

blank state waiting to be filled. Light is sifted through the clouds,
highlights then deflects. Close your eyes. The invisible

saying now, now, 'you', an insect on a lake, a moth on glass,
the stealth of ocean currents, waves that feather in the wind,

the merest touch. You open your mouth to cry and a bird flies out.
Another and another. They arrange themselves in rank and order,

drop like stones. The sea responds with holes. If this is it,
if there is nothing more, then nothing must be more,

what is not cannot be. Hold my hand. We are strange uncertain beasts,
rooted to this place, singing without conviction

until a landscape intervenes. We shrink against the hills,
are lost in the verticals of trees, the clutch and merge of waves,

our voices drowning in this curious light.

"In the hour or so"

In the hour or so before night's certain fall,
as light cuts loose the day and heat relents,
the body recalls what it is to breathe and sometimes
the mind finds pleasure in teeming emptiness.
Today there are no shadows and particulars
are soft with lack of definition. The jacaranda
against the church's mortared, crumbling mass,
mauve and stunning and substantial as it is—
all indirect flowering of twists and turns—
seems uncontained, as though at any moment
it might escape the rooted, understandable restraints
of space and time and float away as weightless
as a dandelion on the emerging evening breeze.

ERIN ENTERMANN

Cathedral

Dedicated to the people of Christchurch,
a city I was once lucky to call home.

A cavern of cold, grey stone.
Space that fills with silence
so large, so grand,
that it isn't silence anymore.

Dawn's ribbons of welcoming light
fall through the painted windows.

The voices of collared children
levitate and swirl.
They fill the once ominous space
with reverent greetings.

Hours pass like this until,
like a wind, one by one
each person leaves.

Returning the Cathedral
to cold, grey stone.

A chamber of austerity.

Ten-Cent Hero

Nineteen past eleven
already two minutes late.
I look across the tracks,
the train is waiting,
threatening to abandon.

Behind scratched and foggy glass
the gruff voice says,

Two dollars and ten cents

I only have two dollars and five

No good to me.

In my startled state,
my thoughts are a blur
and I ask myself
why can't he grant me
five cents grace?

Then unexpectedly,

Here.

I turn to the voice
in simple attire
just shorts and t-shirt,
no remarkable style.

He has a young but weathered face.
And his freckled hands
press into mine
a ten cent piece.

ERIN ENTERMANN

The Moment

He sits
slowly
and pauses.
Hands clasped,
head bowed.

In this moment of calm
you believe it is silent,
but it is not.

There are hushed whispers,
self-conscious coughs
and throat clearings.
The scraping of a chair.

But no-one seems to mind
the disrupting sounds.

They are waiting.

He raises his head
readies his fingers,
poising them,
curving them,
over his shrine.

Every noise ceases
and the air grows tense.

They wait

for his first note.

Kolam

Kolam of a hundred and one eyes
Chalked, closed circuits of eternity
What if you could speak
Like Scheherazade's 1001 nights
Of Stories from *Here, Not There*!

JANE FERNANDEZ

Colours

Long forgotten
These themes of love and sacrifice
Sleeping now amongst the good ghosts!
On the stage here
Rehearsing there—
Children of a lesser god
Pluck at strings—
The sitar is mute
The chamber silent
BUT
the *raga* rises soft and strong
Birthing here
I
Return there
To your colours of saffron and rice

My Birthright

Dedicated to my mother 'Sara'

This is no treasure hunt
Nailing my birthright
In the sand
Like the angelus recitation
From Here to There and Not there
A *memorare* of memories ...
Flowing
Writing
Someone's prayer for the future

JEMMA GALINDO

Frozen

She blows back the door
and barges inside,
sweeps me aside
snow blows on the floor.

The Ice Queen is here,
blinding white in Arctic's dress.
She's pale and sharp,
hair of rain-driven clouds,
South Wind is the cat twining her legs.

Hot and furious, I had been snarling and burning—
but when she turns her glittering
cold glare on me,
words freeze on my lips—
ships trapped in the flows.

She cackles and closes
and cloisters
me.
Blood turns to ice
congeals in my veins.

Bitten by blizzard's venom,
I wrap myself in her royal cloak.
Armoured, cold, silent and tall.

Now I am Her.

The Wind

Tickle, tickle, tickling.
Its fingers tease the leaves and the whole tree trembles.
Then wrapping 'round a leafy head,
It twists away leaving the tree all bare and free.

Rush, rush, rushing.
It sprints up the mountainside and kicks away the pebbles.
Grasps the spindly grasses,
Then releases to catch a cloud, departing swept and hardy earth.

Roar, roar, roaring.
It crushes its fists against the buildings and tears at age-stained tiles.
Conducts the waves in an angry chorus,
Pounds on all that stands before it, breaking away in helpless rage.

Yearn, yearn, yearning.
It swims through sandy fields of grain, searches in an ageless day.
Peers into the crevasse of darkness,
Answerless, it streams away.

Whisper, whisper, whispering.
It curls up on well-worn rock and dreams of future journeys.
Breathes.
And slumbers on in drifting rest 'til next current wakens,
The voices of the wind.

JEMMA GALINDO

This or That

I met a girl the other day who had two sides.
To look at she had a left and a right,
a front and a back.
But what I saw was more a war—
a Germany and France.

She's like that ginger tabby cat,
that looks so proud and stays aloof.
But then you find her under your feet, so loveable,
you wonder why you thought her proud.
Then she stalks away to prove she never cared,
and next she's chasing her tail,
as if never satisfied that it belongs to her.

This side has blue eyes and an easy grin.
On the other side her eyes turn grey and
smiles will never show her crooked teeth.
Spin the marionette and look again:
she waves at the dishes and shrugs
"they'll be there tomorrow."
Next she storms around in a huff
because the floors aren't swept.

Spin it fast enough and the colours blur
and a single one emerges,
but even the cat gets dizzy after a while.
You say the side you see is different,
and therefore what I see is wrong.
And while we argue overhead,
she crumples to the floor—
exhausted from the war.

Black Nectar

I wake to your fragrance
steamy, bold
as I hold you close
I feel the warmth.

That black nectar
sometimes mellowed
with a little creamy love.

As I ask, one spoon or two
of this hot sweetness
your aroma lingers
in the morning air.

Craving that second cup
like an encore,
taking a bow
of aromatic bliss.

BROCK GOODHILL

A Glimpse

Weathered, dirty hands scour through trash
as judgment cracks like lightning around them.
Some feel they are "foulness" fermenting the streets;
damp, brown soil beneath their feet.

Weakened shoulders hang as willows weep;
on lonely nights, eyes cast into fragile dreams.

As seasons change, each line on her face
tells a story of life's hells and glories.
Hungry will work for food, her sign reads…

I will do anything, outstretched hand pleads.

In this dying world, people run through their maze—
blind to other's pain.

Her heart dressed in dark, tattered clothes
is brightened by acts of kindness—
rivers of mercy to one's slipping soul.

If only for a moment, she peers into humbling eyes,
catching just a glimpse of where hope lies.

In Thiele Court, Barker

Wind that moves
the shadows on stone,
that cracks the leaves
and shakes the trees

You speak to me

softly
hesitantly
silently.

Sometimes
when it is summer
and not now
you shake your fist in my face.
You shout at my window
and bang at my door.

The children cower.

The dog runs in for shelter.

But that is then
and this is now.

Now it is autumn
with an azure sky
and leaves largely yellow.

Now there is sunlight
speckling on sails,
and late azaleas,
and white gardenias,

and poets,

and poetry.

KIMBERLEY HODGKIN

Cycling to School with my Sister

For Kylie

We would ride to school like newly hatched turtles determined to make it to sea,
dodging metallic birds who, through no fault of our own,
would swoop and tally yet another near miss.
We'd struggle up the mountainous inclines
then be rewarded with scuttling quickly down the other side.
We were hatchlings who instinctively knew where to go,
exploring the quickest path to our destination, but never getting lost.
Our school was the ocean, calling us to it.

Uneven Distribution

My pizza was stacked the way I like,
toppings heaped high like a mountain I'd hike.
I was so focused on it that I almost didn't see
the outrageous atrocity that was clearly before me.
Though my pizza was big and spacious and round,
I tell you the toppings could only be found
on one of the pieces of pizza, you know,
the rest were bare and naked, just dough.

I couldn't believe it, this wasn't fair!
My pizza should be covered, not mostly bare.
You told me this pizza would be good,
was there something I misunderstood?
There are plenty of toppings to cover the base
so why were they heaped all in one place?
I just want a pizza that's covered evenly—
It's not that hard if you ask me.

FERGUS HOGAN

Watching Clouds

I watch the clouds
And think of you
As once we did together

How they change
From day to day and hour to hour
Like you, and me I guess

They too seem to move
From mass to space
And then evaporate

Garden Days

The garden is alive with Beauty
And I want to give it all to you

A daisy a day
And a buttercup under your chin

Red poppies like sails in the sunset
To swim us away together

Let me remember
Gentle days

When all we had was
Time and Love

Grassplay
Skyshapes

Sometimes the world opens up
And smiles upon us

Sometimes we are closer to Nature
Sometimes She is closer to us

CAROL JENKINS

In Loco Parentis

Sky claxon, sleep stealer, winging into any nest.
Pest. Egg bowler, orphan-layer, ruckus-maker,
who crimps dawn's silence into bar rests for the next.

Interloper, striped insinuator, you're the nemesis
of decent nestlings, the betrayer of hapless hosts:
fig bird, oriole, honey-eater and spangled drongo.

Guilty party of the broken home, head-ache-er,
curse-originator, cause of canopy cacophony
despicable delegator, cuckoo of another rule.

Silkweeds

It seems simple and I trust the weight of silk—
the strands' flat lustre that flattens into slub
then regularises as yarn,
laid under, over, in plain weave,
the colour's flax, honey, straw, *raw silk* they say,
—the two words work together
so silk takes all the rawness out of raw.

The fabric glows as if inside the threads
silkworms are reading poetry by lamp light,
couchant in their cocoons. In the dream,
I am wearing a skirt I never had,
explaining that, *No, I didn't make it, I can't sew*,
and to demonstrate reveal how the clever seamstress
over-locked the raw edge of flat cut pleats,
and in this dream I believe this manifesto
so absolutely, its moth wings beat
exultant against the inside of my ribs.

But the next morning, and maybe for ever after,
I compare these two contrary weeds:

the dream where silk is skirt and I aver—*I know*—
I am unable to sew;
and the raw silk trousers, worn and made by me,
revived by this dream's sartoriality,
these true ghosts, two decades old.

Varuna Dreaming

dedication to Eleanor Dark

She dreams of words and timeless places.
She dreams of lands and people
and traces
their lives in her dreaming.

The other is Dark
and watches and hears
from above the hearth
and through the years
(they form no barrier):
the same bird call
as I.

The trees are greater now than when she saw—
ten years more.
The birds the ancestors
of hers.

But the Fall sun
streaming
in is the one
of her dreaming.

And mine—

the red, the ochre, the burgundy,
the same;
the golden green scents lingering
after the rain;
her window a frame
to the Blues of the Mountain
mirrored high—
the heraldic sky.

Storm cloud shadowing across her lawn.

Cool breeze whispering of frost already born—
of time—
already on its way.

The Autumn day.

The same.

She smiles
not with her lips.
With her eyes,
and is calm.

She sighs,
still here in The Studio

Dreaming
with me.

***

UNIA JUMA

Bones

In the heart
of the East African savannah bushes
a child squats.

In her dusty dark skin
she is a stick figure
with a swollen stomach.
She screams silently
in the scorching
heat that has turned
the lush meadow
yellow, dry and brown.

She lies on the parched soil,
her vision blurs and her saliva
dries as she watches the orange sunset.

Train Tracks

In church, scorning eyes
pierce my dignity.
Waves of whispers whir—

Look at what she is wearing!
Is she living on taxpayers' money?

So called church elders—
more like Pharisees.

Arriving home,
the vibrant colours of gerberas
alleviate their censorious voices.

My gaze draws its focus
past the fence to the train tracks.
They lure me,
they shimmer like silver
and shine like a sharpened blade.

BRIDGET KEATING

A Letter to my Daughter

Before your birth,
I carve your eyes,
the creases in your hands,
the ridges of your fingertips.

Cut bone to sculpt you from my body.

I gather shale
splintered rock
layered silt
to create memory.

The land offers you stories,
stains you with gleyed soil.

You are born on the day of the Revolution.
A head crowned with lights.

Matted down
damp wrinkled skin.
Eyes black pearls
cultured in womb.

Birthed from this charnel house,
blood and bone of ancestors,
weight of history,
body blanketed with marrow,
tongue stitched with stories.

Malintzin's blood flows through your veins.

This woman of grass,
mythical Nahua mother,
claims you as her daughter.

Swaddles your body in woven cloth,
kisses your face with ruby lips.
whispers in your ear.

Tells tales of cities with streets of silver and floating gardens.
Of women who wear thick masks,
their teeth painted.

They dance with forked heron feathers in the *cuicalli.*
Feast on maize. Drink *pulque.*

She tells you of the children who sleep
beneath blankets filled with quills and gold powder,
their necks lined with jade beads.

They celebrate your arrival with gifts
of stones and clay.

It was then that Itzpapalotl,
the clawed butterfly,
came for you.

Cursed with fingers fashioned from sculpted metal stakes,
she longed to hold you,
clutched you between her lips,
carried you away to Tamoanchan,
the burial grounds of your ancestors.

There, she left you in the furrow of a tree,
its blood nectar nourishing you
until you grew with such strength and knowledge
that from your web of silk
scaled wings became your arms
and antennae your eyes.

In Tamoanchan,
you saw the others—
chrysalids woven in gold thread,

their bodies emerging
in the early morning light.

They, too, were taken
and, from ground bones and spilled blood,
borne anew.

By this time,
your skin had darkened,
and your hair,
long and unbound,
woven with acanthus leaves,
fell to your waist.

You stained your face with yellow and red
and set out to gather pebbles of agate and chalcedony,
drawn by the singing of the dead.

Do you remember this long passage?
It was marked with such silence
that, soon after,
words left us.

The stories no longer fell from tongues
but were carried, weightless and without meaning,
by the force of the wind,
and swallowed by the strength of the sky.

And what was left was interred quietly beneath the ground.

Sparrows

My son says
no one ever notices sparrows.

They are not pretty like other birds,
and they annoy people.

Through the kitchen window
we watch them,
thin winter bodies
birthed from branches of elm trees.

He tells me
they carry the souls of the dead
on their wings,
and clutch in stubbed beaks
souls of newborns from the sky.

My son, his quiet hunger,
body thirsting for attention,
understands this journey.

I carried him once,
a stone in my fertile belly
grew flesh and bone.

His arms became wings,
took flight.

He feels the sparrows' breath when they sing,
quiet songs gripped in earth's gut
rising from silt and rock beneath his feet.

JEAN KENT

In the Middle of the Night in the Wrong Part of the World (Paris)

I wake and think the street is whispering
with rain—but rain falls silently here,
it oozes down buildings from a grey sponge sky,
no tin roof to receive it, no wind to hurl it silver
against window glass. Blindly I walk
toward this gentle storm, feel the ice
of double glazing against my face as the softly chittering
truck on the cobbles below revs up
and passes on. For a moment I am almost under a pale sky
holding only half a dozen spilt-milk stars.

Still, alert, disappearing where I stand—
like a shy wallaby at dusk, I look out.
Against my skin this other
country's curtains

turn soft as old paperbark, peeling back.

The Language of Light

(from '*Le Weekend* in Paris')

Weekends, Paris walks. Something shifts
underground. Like a Rubik's cube
slightly twisted
the lines of colours realign, the harmony of humans
gently shudders the city's symmetrical grid.

Like the still spaces we enter when music
moves us, weekends separate us from the deafness
of habitual days. More so than ever
here, on the other side
of our usual world—
here, where we live lit up
like cymbals always on the verge
of being struck. In the Luxembourg Gardens
I am one small vibration in the shivering of the city
toward some Sunday song. The babble of all the world
is being quietened here

Poles and Italians, Australians and Africans,
small boys and motorised boats all blend into a buzz
swarming from under the acid-yellow horse-chestnut leaves
toward the end of summer's silver
hived within the lake.

Weekends, Paris talks with less tension
accelerating its tongue. Even the tourist buses—
clattering to halts like the abruptly dropped snakepods
of bauhinia trees—
release people who become, after a little time here,
as calm as seeds
waiting to be planted. We almost believe

we could all belong—as we settle briefly
on these wrought-iron chairs with their ringletted arms
and verdigris-barred backs. We subside

on seats tattooed all over with holes
spraying sunlight onto the crushed white gravel below.
How many faces
have fallen here—
waiting for Paris light to persuade them
to float back up, to lift
towards it their first foreign shoots?

Weekends, Paris walks. It stalks us—as gently
as the grandparents we never knew, those ghosts
who passed through a war here
eighty years ago.
Like the nano-shifting of volcanic plates now,
something in us shifts. Whatever homes we thought
we had brought with us
settle like hidden pockets
in our winter coats—and we join the long lines
of stilled people in black swivelling towards

the slightest caress of sun. The light,
as it negotiates peace settlements
within this temporary country
of cold shoulders,
is speaking everyone's ancestral tongue.

It Begins with Darkness

People file into the room, find their seats,
fill up the air with chatter. The stage
is bare except for a leather couch
and a lamp on a chrome and bakelite stand.
It's meant to be an old factory converted
to an apartment—exposed pipes, a ceiling
fit for a cathedral, polished oak floorboards.
A man dressed in black makes an announcement
about mobile phones. The lights go down.
I don't know what I'm doing here,
I just know that this is theatre, my son an actor.

I hear his voice before I see him. It's as loud
as the wind swatting at a loose sheet of corrugated iron
on the chook shed. When he comes on stage
he swears five times in the first minute,
all in the presence of a lady. I've a good mind
to go down and slap him about the face,
except that I'm sitting right in the middle of the row
and it wouldn't be easy getting past all those knees.
Then I remember that he's pretending
to be someone else, that this is his job now.
Soon everyone is laughing—they're smiling
and nodding and taking in every move my son makes.

I've never been to a play before. It's not
boilermaking, not the flying sparks from an arc welder,
not the precision required for a submarine hull,
nor the relief of taking off your helmet,
gloves and apron and enjoying the coolness
of a harbour breeze as you eat your lunch,
but it is, I guess, a different kind of trade.
I watch more and it all happens before my eyes
and I can see that he loves this lady,
everyone can see it and I want to say, "Son,

what are you afraid of?" I want to reach out
and lift him up as I did when he was two
years old, riding a supermarket trolley
and screaming as if he'd just discovered
the power of his lungs. But I can't touch him now
or even talk to him and I have this feeling
that it will turn out badly, like the week you have
the numbers in Lotto, but forget to buy the ticket.

The stage is dark again and he's not swearing now
and the lady's really pleased to see him
and she burns this scrap of paper and it flares up,
bright and yellow in the darkness
and the flame flickers across his forehead
and I glimpse in my son's face the unmistakable
features of my father who is ten years dead.
Although the three of us won't ever meet again,
I'm sure Dad would have loved this—a story
that takes a whole evening in the telling
and a small fire that leaps and glows
and transfixes us, for as long as it burns.

Flight

Sometime in June or July, throw on a cable-stitched
grey jumper or even a thick coat for warmth,
take the afternoon off and head out past Kurnell
to Cape Solander. There, on the white sandstone cliffs
above the vast sprawl of the sea, look
for humpbacks heading north, swimming near the shore
to dodge the ocean current sliding south.
Witness, if you're lucky, a whale breaching—
the corrugated whiteness of its wobbly ascension,
the dark certainty and blazing glitter of its fall.
The cold breeze ruffles the diamond quilt
until it's as messy as an unmade bed, it tugs
at the waving tendrils of spear grass and at the tips
of your ears, it makes your eyes water
as if some old sadness has unexpectedly taken hold.
You can find no sign of a sea eagle, hovering;
you cannot name the endangered species
growing in this headland heath. But you can close
your eyes, you decide to do this simple thing,
electing to completely miss the whale if it rises again,
aware now of this immense, unknown life
going on around you, within you, as the buffeting,
lunging wind picks you up and gives you wings.

RICHARD LANDER

Quorrobolong Sunset

"Foo" like, the sun lowers its forehead behind the Watagan Range
Puffy clouds, 'Foo's' fingers, dip below the saw-tooth
Cutting night from day
Evening incandescence is slowly dimmer-switched into submission
Mighty eucalypts,
Just moments before white-trunked and strong
Now mere black lacework against the evening sky
It, in time, becomes all pinks and greys,
A galah with wings spread wide
Frogs chirruping in crescendos like the heartbeat of this ancient bush
Theirs the only sound.

Greys

There should be a word for subtle
beyond the clumsiness of categories. I am thinking
of the silver-, black- and buff-inflected greys
of a nondescript country of bloodwoods and apples,
geebung and silver-top ash; so nondescript—
what gulfs of arrogance—it is almost invisible.
Just a copse, and then a copse, and then another.
There is no central grey to which others relate.
There is only an angled abundance of juxtapositions.
But cloud warmth is in them. They are at home
in sun, glinting and settled in spectra. They're at home
in monstrous sheet-blue and in light, shifting airs.
Coded for dull, they are intricate, various, endless,
dishevelled, complete. Ochre and pale-yellow laminates
glow underneath them. Brilliant black tesserae
scroll them with fire-scars: flame-welts of charcoal
down cork-stubborn, low-relief ziggurats. More than
defined by, they grow out of weather: rain-swell
and wind-tug, regular sun-pressure thickenings;
seasons that summon and glide
with the tremulous shadows-and-lace of their noons.

If we must have a flag, these are the greys
I would have there: subtleties, plenitudes,
at home in vast, even light;
none more important than others, with no grey more visible;
space all around them, and through them, and on either side—
a welcome, without exclusivities;
a scuffed, twiggy opening you enter with every next step.

MARTIN LANGFORD

The Dragonfly

The layers of rock to the southwest of Sydney
were tilted and raised in as long as it takes
for a dragonfly's flight to change tack.
The wings made the faintest of hums.
The clear, braided streams from the mountains
bore coarse grains to Camden and Lithgow;
round Gosford up north. While dragonflies mated,
the ground to the north-east was lifted.
The rivers from south-west, the rivers from north-west,
kept laying down grains, building ply.

While mandibles sliced through a gnat,
the lazy Nepean was gouging its way through the strata.
A dragonfly hung like a sapphire
while Lapstone reared west and the river slid east.
The sea-level rose and eased back
like adjustments in hover. The suck and dilation
of glass exchanged ground with the trees.
Streams carved through echoes of spinebills.
The Port Jackson shark and the mulloway
nosed into gullies. A dragonfly glinted like language.
It gleamed like the seepage
and unweathered stone of a rock-fall. Like mica in sun.

Flower

for Nicholas Little, my father

Your *little flower*
I was growing up fast
But winter came—
its cold tendrils crept into my life
And took yours away.

Just a little bud
my roots not yet deep.
The soil frozen
from too much cold
almost burning me.

Then the sunshine returned.
Not quite as bright.
A flower I am, and growing still
but cautious of winter
returning too soon.

ANNE LITTLE

The Ocean

"I am big enough," I said,
I can go out there!
Just a little girl the youngest of all,
I wanted to join.

I paddled out, my arms getting tired
but on and on I pushed.
I could see them out the back of the waves
like little specks of dust in the distance.

Finally I reached them
where the water was still as glass.

Now my mum is a speck of dust on the shore
I can see her arm waving like a little flag,
calling us back.

"We'd better go back in," my brother says.
I try to keep up but I am just too small.
My board is drifting out to sea
everyone else is taken in
by a helpful wave

My heart is humming like a birds' wings.
Suddenly I see
my big brother has come back.

He grabs my board and I feel like a ship being tugged along.
The shore is coming closer.
Relief washes through me as I see my mother.

Never again will I try to be bigger than I am.

Bylands Farm

Running down the hill the grass whipping at their legs
Quickly! Quickly! They must make it to their place
to the bottom where they always play.

Three little girls, more sisters than friends,
flit around the farm like three little wrens.
Down the bottom of the hill,
they creep up quietly.

The trees droop down like girls' hair,
they curtain them from the outside world.
The frogs croak deeply from the pond—
the buzz, busily working away bees.

The breeze picks up,
the smell of cow dung stings their noses,
the familiar scent brings peace.
This is their home.

LYNNETTE LOUNSBURY

A Night of Deep Thought and Soft Pillows

We move so far from the wet air of whimsy,
that all seems too clear
and too sharp most of the time,
too real and brittle edged and everyday
and when it wraps us in its fog of rich truth
and lifts us those few precious feet
from the ground, we sigh and whine for its brevity
and its sparse redolent wine,
and we clamber back to earth simply
so we can cringe at the everyday all over again.
Is there not enough of art to lift us fully, hourly, ever?
Surely there is rich coffee and dark poetry enough
for life to be mostly in the brume,
mostly above detergent and floss and rather
filled with the heat of lascivious nothing.

Mobile Phone

Car door shuts
Kilometres hum by on the expressway.
Wait a minute
Where are you?
Did I leave you behind?
The day cannot begin!
My palms are moist
There's a lump in my throat, or is it breakfast?
One hand on the wheel
The other fumbling.
Calculator, camera, credit cards—
Yes! Finally your rectangular smooth feel.

We had started so well
I bought a plan
But you have confined me
Made my car an office
With electronic windows.
You draw me like a magnet
I tremble at your beckoning.
Dare me to leave you behind!
I'll do it! I mean it!
Who's that?
I'll pull over.

HELENE LOW

My Mother's Hands

I remember my mother's hands
strong and hard,
work instruments that constantly strummed her life,
they could easily have been a man's.

They tirelessly gathered the frozen fallen olives,
picked the field in one day, for the wages of a litre of oil.

Today they are twisted and gnarled like twigs, bundled together
as they wash clothes, dishes, floors.
Buttons they hate.

They fumble to hold coins that slip through gaps,
so frustrated she gives notes.
Bundle them to receive coins.

I have never held them, nor have they held me.

Unprivileged hands that fight for life,
"Help me" is not in their vocabulary.

Moment in Japan

Red, black and white
Koi carp in a pool
thick green moss
paving the sloping ground
granite rocks sparkling
in the sunlight
red maple leaves
falling softly
the red tide flowing
slowly
down the slope

do not hurry

please do not hurry.

RANDY LUNDY

Birthday Poem

November again—

the going down, going away, going beyond
time.
Your birth month,
Dear Scorpio.

Your Mother's and your Father's clasped hands
float like constellations above your head.

November again—

mid-summer's apple blossoms, the susurration of deep green leaves
breathing wind,

two white dogs asleep in afternoon shade,
cigarette smoke whisked away, the closest thing to cloud,

when the breeze subsides, the smoke hangs like stratocumulous
just before rain,

a garden of river-rock and burnished, fire-bellied volcanic stone
hears the call of thunder,
aches to respond,

wolf-willow, juniper, and sage ebullient beneath lightning,
in the cone-flowers, the saturated euphony of bees,

humid midnight walk on the grid road, gravel crunching beneath
a pair of cheap hikers that will leave your feet blistered,

the moon distant,

the stars close, Sirius, Dog Star,
inviting coyote songs,

the far-off whistle-response of a train—

all of this nothing but memory now, useless,
detritus,
nothing more than distraction.

Isn't the journey of the mind toward perfection
simply the clearing away of distractions?

The transit of the earth
the slight tilt of its axis
has given you this, has birthed you into this season—

the silent time, time for your mind to lustrate
in the dark hours,
with the sinuate, anabiotic trees.

Fogged in, early-winter morning, moccassins and tea, thirteen snow-geese,
low, but barely visible, like the winter-sun, overhead.

Let your mind follow them into the fields where they will feed
on the tiny fists of frozen seeds left over from harvest.

A few grey afternoon hours of no-mind will do you good.
Have your books and your bath.

At the end of the day,
calligraphed by winter wind, perhaps slightly less hungry than when it left,
your mind will return for your body's climb up the carpeted stairs, the lying down,
the final inhalation and exhalation, and the exultation of another release

into sleep, into dream
into languages other than your own—

the November-night wind comes from every direction,
curls its ten thousand tongues around the corners of your house,
buffets the eaves, slips beneath the door, seeps in at the windows,

in your ear it speaks, saying,

Happy Day of Birth, Happy Season of Birth,
Oh My Nameless One, Oh My Unnamable Son.

Letters

A box of old letters
sits on a shelf.

Some days they are remembered
and others

left alone.

Gently, two hands bring it down
to recall the faded images

one by one.

An envelope, brown with age,
pushed back into its place.

Its message would bring back that feeling
and that can't be felt again.

Another letter,
so carefully

set aside.

It brought a smile.

CHARNELLE MACK

Lying

Curled up on the lawn
in that sunny spot,
dreaming of yesterday's journey
from flowers, through hedge,
to grass.

Long and slender,
smooth to touch,
slithers as it moves

here and there in warmer months,
flaunting green,
or black, or stripes.

But more often than not,
in its place on the lawn,
the garden hose is napping
by the old rusty tap.

Morning Abyss

I step outside.
It is cold, and dark.
I am alone.

The chills of the autumn morning run deep into my bones.
They shiver in constant rhythm in order to survive.
I can smell the dew upon the grass.
The bite of the winter air leaves my mouth dry, with very little taste.
As I take a step further I can see the fog rising.

I hear nothing.

My view is desolate, as if every animal knows its place at this hour.
As I walk further out, the green foggy mist soaks through my skin.

There is still something missing.

Amongst this private and self-sufficient life,
I sometimes long for another person.
I wait for the morning to come, to see another out pondering their thoughts.
Someone who feels that time is like a python,
waiting to crush the diaphragm of anyone who comes in its path.
Someone who knows that time is a gun,
and we don't pull its trigger.

I turn around.

And for the first time, I see you there.

BRITTANY McNITT

The Spectator's Nightmare

It was a black August night.
The room was dark, empty,
but this emptiness was not seen, only felt.

It was as if the room had taken on his physical being.
It was as if it knew the events the night would bring.

It was full of voices, but the silence was screaming,
as its echoes pounded off the walls.

I could leave the room if I wanted,
but he could not.
It was his cell we stood in.
It was his finish we watched.

The ticking clock was counting more than just time.
It was counting his every gasp,
every gasp for air.

His skin was dry, like the taste in my mouth.
I watched his chest rise and fall.
His lips quivered as if to say he was trying to hold on.

His inhalations grew shorter,
and the seconds ticked faster.

I wanted to vanish back to my youth,
when my summer felt endless and the world was a playground.
But I was stuck in this desolate room
with a heart that felt heavier than a rock with a rope
falling into the ocean.

And as the lump sank in my chest
I could hear death's voice,
like needles in my ears
scratching at the surface as they found their way inside.

Musician's Interruption

He sits
on that hard weathered stool
Fingers perched
on the ivory blocks like a bird
ready to
sing
before it soars

Taking the plunge
his hands
    lead
Every note chasing
the
upcoming
sounds

The rhythm
of each new movement
matches
the pulsing
of his
inner
master

The world blares in
            Slowing

His eyelids linger, then
    fall
as droplets after rain

BENJAMIN MILIS

Pinhole

I woke up to the guilty ignorance of my alarm. Bounded out of bed, knocking the Mozart on my bedside to a kind of second death. Case of the disappearing sock. Opened the fridge but the Up&Go was the only choice. I slammed the car door shut on my leg. Unbelievable, the traffic you experience in Cooranbong. All because of that old bird and her cat that cross Alton when it best suits them. Did I mention that I ran late to harmony class after finding five missed calls and four inspiring voicemutters? Received a hair in my lunch burger, found a spare minute for the restroom, then continued writing the production script as I trudged to week-evening ensemble frenzy. Completely frazzled, I now stand in my driveway, eyes fixed to the night blanket above me. Awe strikes my entire being as I spin around and realise that my life is but a mere pinhole of light amongst the millions.

[Body] for Rent

Her book was sold
for the cover art.

Her book was thumbed through
for it was fresh
written not spoken
with a heady bouquet of pages.

Her book was sold
not to be read
but to rent.

Her book was abused
for it was judged by its blurb.

Her book was spread open
bookmarked and ribboned
without being read.

Her book bled
ink trickling soon clotting.

Then her book was
s
t
r
i
p
p
e
d
down to only one page of ink.

Still nobody was there to read to her.

Onion

James lived in his giant peach.

My giant onion
lived in me.

James made friends with humanlike insects in his peach.

My giant onion
made friends with my two-way choice between Asia and the Pacific.

James' friend Centipede said he had one hundred legs.

My giant onion
had almost one hundred layers of thought to peel through.

James' friends thought about squashing his aunties with his peach.

My giant onion
thought my friends would squash the layers, and me.

James' peach put people in a panic.

But I kept peeling back the layers of my giant onion, and the next layer always gave me the same answer.

My giant onion
held my thoughts like a mushy peach, yet the layers were set.

It showed me where in the world to go.

Ripples

What is the number of water?
As many as the ripples going nowhere
across the surface of the pond.

I've counted them in my ear
and on my fingers. Scanned by wind,
they rise out of nothing,

roofing the pool with see-through tiles
that slide away from where
they were, from where the action was

to where they go: a steady ticking
off into nothing, cool sines
fluttering the axis at the pool's lip.

Every now and then the air
damages the water with graphs
of gooseflesh, but then the liquid grooves

resume their count, marching lines
that rise and dip:
as many as I am and more, much more.

DAVID MUSGRAVE

Watermark

Never judge a book by its reader
unless it's the kind that's read as if by touch,
fingers skimming down the columns
as if shutting dead eyes. The language
in that book requires no translation
other than what it becomes, which is itself
plus desire. The days are flowing messily
as money; but without the usual muddle:
every drop accounted for, like how a puddle,
stamped on, sneaks back to form before
another step. If the earth is alive
the oceans are its eye. In another's hands,
the book is something else. Hold up to the light
the note, the stamp and it will bear witness.

Tapestry

for Roland Robinson

You open your book,
Turn on the lamp.
I reach for my tapestry.
The needle flashes

Fire that flares on
The crimson cushion,
Ricochets from
The glazed bowl,

Leaps in conflagration
Up the stand of flowers
You gave me—
Those tall carnations.

You flick over
Λ pagc, and, slowly,
I pull through
The shining thread.

VERA NEWSOM

Orchid Moon

I had no fire in my hand,
no orchid flame,
till you walked the headland
at Seal Rocks,
saw the full moon
flooding the rock cleft
where the sea boils.

Now rain drowns the moon,
lightning pierces the chasm,
your body recoils in terror;
but I hold fast
its angular tree,
earthing the shock.
O my lightning conductor.

I have never seen those smooth seals
rise from the ocean;
but out of my earth,
through my fingers, fire leaps;
the bulb of the old moon splits
and over the headland the night orchid
sprouts its horns.

Happiness

Happiness as a landscape is
a pleasant plain, a low plateau
with a slight slope here and there
for a gentle view
of fields and cows and one
encouraging far-off spire.

Happiness as a house is
a modest size
with geraniums at the sill,
and by the door, a family
of shoes lined-up, and a little cat
fur left on the welcome mat.

Happiness as a dance
is not a tango, not a dervish spin,
hardly a jig,
more like
a circle dance over again
after the maypole's gone.

Happiness as a feeling is
an undertaking
with props and supports, crutches even:
on a little low table,
paper and pen whose infant words begin
'happiness is a pleasant plain.'

JAN OWEN

At the Persian Palace

The floor was a patchwork carpet
of festive cemetery plots
in basket-weave—
rubaiyats of colour,
back alleys of jasmine and musk.
The walls exhaled bright pelts
or stilled to dim stained glass
formal and sad
as the silk-browed owner
who flipped through pile after pile,
his tired obsession.
One thousand and one
swap cards, dog-eared.
He was opening a wound in time
with the muscle flap hard to hold back:
This, very fine, from Isfahan,
this one from Qum and this,
Madame, from Shiraz.
Towns under towns—
ruby stains, amethyst shards, topaz.
In the intimate quiet
that grows before a sale
he smoothed a kashkai down
like a counterpane.
She chose a prayer-mat,
crimson, scarlet, white, black-flecked,
with roses, tendrils, urns
and zig-zag paths:
a garden seen through a glass of wine
but steady as bread,
a flat unleavened loaf with a scatter of seed.

Raspberries

for Derwent and Daphne

The warmth of the sun
kisses my back, and my toes
dangle in the crisp cool creek.
It's late summer— raspberry season.

Soon back at the house, I dally in the garden,
its rows bulging with
cherries, mangoes, pineapples and berries.

But it's the raspberries that hold my attention.

Their small red bodies so delicious,
one bite, and I'm home.
Held by hands—
stained red with love.

Day in, day out you'll find me
beside the laden vines,
the berries poised
to colour my mouth a blissful scarlet.

But all too soon I know the vine will turn brittle,
the leaves golden.
The berries will fall, their overripe juices and bruised bodies
splatting on the ground.

But now I'm static, poised.

What will I do when the raspberries are gone?

NIKARRI PARKER

Running

My vision narrows, the forest
blurs into abstract green.
No distinction between
shrubs, trunks, trees and sticks.

The buds in my ears pump
the melody my feet dance to.
My heartbeat is
a staccato overlay.

Run away from me baby, run away.
Run away from me baby, run away.

As I run there is no before or after,
only now.

My world is
a series of bends,
'when you reach that one, you'll be halfway'
I trick my mind.

I'm bulletproof, nothing to lose,
fire away, fire away.

My feet pound the dirt and rocks
mud squelches and sticks snap,
but the beat keeps going,
and so do I.

You shoot me down, but I won't fall,
I am TITANIUM.

Almost there.

My eyes focus on the final bend,
one more,
one more

How Time Passes

for Ruby and Coco

time passes
I stare
the wind blows
there is no sign of you coming
I feel bare

time passes
I jump
the sun shines
my heart skips two beats
there are two lines
I feel joy

time passes
I hear your beats
a photo of blur, black and white swoosh
a promise
such promise
your promise

time passes
I am stretched
my heart is too
you kick, nudge, tap
I am coming

time passes
I hear footsteps, or skipping
no—running

Here you are

CAROLYN RICKETT

Colouring

After you died we could not (perhaps would not) use
dark pens of any kind because they felt inked
with the same-skinned bruise that spread
and spread its way to pages soiled and stalled.

Even the garden violets—small contusions—planted
only with your name in mind seemed so
untouchably and unreachably blue.

Some botanical pedants might strictly argue purple,
but no matter about splitting the palate here—
for the sake of those who still wish to paint
or write you into view, let us simply say
flowers

"A cold coming we had of it"

a re-visitation of T.S. Eliot's 'The Journey of the Magi'

You probably wouldn't choose
our discipleship.
I mean, you just wouldn't.

You might choose
the one of us,
but not the group of us.
Certainly not the whole sorry
lot of us.

Maybe the dog if the day
was fine—if the trip was short.
She wouldn't sit still long enough
for any grand pilgrimage
for royalty not likely.

But if you really pressed and pinched us
we'd go of course. To take the presents.
If the guilt was wrapped thick enough,
we'd load the car. Always do
for the guilt of it.

And grandma like salted Lot's wife
(only she can move an arm)
waves us off with *cheerio*
as the car's obligation scrapes
the cold concrete drive with
our reluctant departure.

I would be sitting
in the front of course
flicking the Gregorys
for a quick and sure sighting
of Bethlehem in the index.

CAROLYN RICKETT

Not here.
(How can you lose a city?)
It's gotta be there dad says
still believing quite
wonderfully in maps.

My brother snatches
over upholstered seats
divining the written compass
for patterns he thinks only
he can see.

Past the Westfield, the golf course,
Kmart and miles and miles of
the blackened Hume.
It's not listed.
The back seat priest finally
pronounces the benediction
of the lost.

We'd tried to avoid the
folly of following a star,
the shabby group of awe-filled
shepherds having long left us
at the BP diner.

Left us murmuring about
the fuel consumption of
the Commodore while they
kept walking their way
to keen salvation.

Directionless dad now says
We'll make record time
don't you worry about that.

The three ordained presents
(gold, myrrh and Tupperware)
sit shakily under my bare feet,
under the mandarin pips, pith
and frond of orange skins.

We hurtle on past
the last driver reviver
past the angelic host
past celestial light
past grace
amazing or otherwise.

We've stopped asking
are we nearly there yet.

The single star
never close never far
tells us something
of the road we're on.

That stretch of false equilibrium
between pot-holed hope and
the manger of a Messiah
not yet found.

NOEL ROWE

Widow of Beijing

The widow of Nain
had it easy: all she had to suffer, after Christ
convinced her son the grave was only joking, was the fear
that if she grabbed his hand too hard
she might interrupt his bones
before they got their second wind.

Here the soldiers fired as they came,
bullets, even though the young had made their hopes
of styrofoam. After a while only blood escaped,
crawling by its elbows, not looking back

to see along the Avenue of Eternal Peace
well-fed flames playing leap-frog in the trees,
playing not unlike children,

as tanks turn bodies over, mashing them,
as dozers shovel into the fire
big, awkward spoonfuls.

So little bone left, the flames don't even feel a scratch.

On this Winter Morning

for Stephen Fahey

On this winter morning, your bare
shoulders shawled by wind, you walk
among your backyard plants and talk
about the healing mantra you have drawn as prayer.

I think about your Buddhist way of art,
its tiny kindling lines, then remember what you said
years ago: "Beauty can be appreciated
only by the empty heart."

Now, on the back step, where the sun is setting
down like monks to meditation,
we see your first orchids flowering.

Sunshine and saffron in the shape of tongues. Yet we recognise,
where each orchid has its crimson break, an old relation,
almost friend, keeping hold: desire's wound and way for being wise.

SOFÍA RUIZ

Birth

I was joyful
I was in my place, protected
floating lightly
to the soft and melodic rhythm of her voice

Suddenly her melodies became screams
stabbing my ears
ripping
deep

Huge pressure took over
consuming me
I was upside down

Gravity held me hostage
and would not let me go

Someone was pulling me down
I felt myself falling
I felt myself dying

My place, which has been so safe
was not anymore
I wanted to scream at the top of my lungs
Save me

And when her cry ceased
mine started

And I breathed
for the first time

And they put me in her arms
for the first time

And she kissed me
for the first time

And I did not die
I started to live

SOFÍA RUIZ

December

I wish you could be here again
right now,
to make me smile.

Distract me for a moment
give me that feeling you get when you look up
no clouds in the sky
and you're eating a chocolate ice-cream.

Bring your warm touch
just for a day
and take me away from this cold winter
I know it can't last long, but I want to
feel at home again.

I want your bright and burning midday sun over my head
the soft breeze that makes the grass sway
the unbearable heat and the glowing, grey sand
next to the freezing, deep blue ocean.
Summer scent.

Bring along my family,
my friends,
my dog,
Christmas, my birthday
and my favourite TV show.

Months seem an eternity
I just can't wait for you,
December.

Naming You

The desire, the yearning, the pleads
Consistent, desperate, measured
Trying
Tiring
Stressful
Wondering
One year. Tick.
Two years. Tick. Tick.
One line. Sigh. Sniff.
One line still. Sigh. Sniff. Pray.

Two lines. Scream. Cry. Jump. Clap.
The real, fast, loud … truly magical
Heartbeat
Tiring
Joyful
Wondering
One month. Tick.
Six months. Move.
Nine months. Come.
Son. Brother. Miracle baby.

Jayden J - God has heard.

SARA THOMPSON

Last Dance

The wind makes us rush—
wind that tears at our clothing and pinned-back hair,
rain that streaks our brushed-up faces
and darkened eyes
till we scramble through backstage doors like shaggy dogs,
wet and stringy, more inclined to shake ourselves off,
than to twirl and spin.

We struggle, each into our own new skins
fitted for us, but not of ourselves;
creations of sequins and tulle
to tell tales
as real as diamonds in the dust.

We feel the call, the whimsical pull
that draws us
into the wings.
Tapping Pointe shoes in rosin, padding
over slippery wooden floors, to wait
poised behind curtains,
gazelles ready to spring
when the spotlights call our names.

But we are a myth
vanishing, quick as a morning mist.
And when the lights die down, we retreat
to the shadows;
as lasting as paper roses
carried away on the breeze.

Shadow Play

I am your ghost
silent, lurking, lest you
turn your

eyes towards me. For I
am earthbound.
Seen, not felt
your hidden self, the
face

of your fears—
yet I am not your enemy.
I dance
to the

rhythm of your song,
leaping in the
sun;

wilting to a mist
in the clouds of grey.
Do not despise me.
Set me free,
and
let

me
Soar.

For
the shadows

of yourself
are the weightless watchers,
the rise and
fall;

the secrets you cannot leave
behind
you.

For without me, you are

nothing.

MARK TREDINNICK

Let Morning Come

1. Hanging on...

A comma is to a poet, of course, what a breath is to a yogi, and for much
the same reason. And the morning looks like she's breathing easy enough,

so I sit beside her at the table that used to be the barn door and which—
unhinged these days, but slimmer—rests up near the house doing nothing

perfectly well in all kinds of imperfect weather, and I try to find nothing
to do. Wearing today his proper name and raiment, the blue-winged king-

fisher lands on one of the tired and sanctimonious digits of those Sad-
ducees, the silver poplars by the cowshed. He takes a moment to reset

his moral compass then turns and throws me a look as stern as a line
from one of my grandfather's sermons. The wind swells like a chord

from a small pipe organ in the temple of the word, and the bird flies
to his pastoral work across the thirsty catchment of the Wingecarribee.

I could get out the gear, I guess, and roll another coat of whitewash
on the ceiling of the shed; I could make another run at the examined life.

But now, above me in the Osage Orange, a single sulphur-crested
cockatoo, white as a lie, prim as a spinster, pins down one ripe green fruit

like prey. She sips the acrid latex as if it were sweet tea and swallows
half the flesh she flenses from the body. The other half she showers down:

so many post-it notes peeled from so much perfect body copy. Soon I'll be
walking those second thoughts inside on the soles of my unknowing boots.

2. … While letting go

The morning, though, sits comfortably in her skin. A little light haze in the east
is the least you'd expect in the wake of a night like last. Did the stars move

for you, too, my love? The white moths are out shopping early. One buzzes
a yellow dandelion and sucks at speed and slows and pivots and spies her mate

by the hedge and flies to him, as though she were in no kind of hurry at all,
and she's fooling no one but herself. I could kiss *you* on the mouth and see

where that got us, if you were not half way home already. And I could start
to miss you, if I hadn't started that in the beginning. Or I could sit and watch dust

rise and run north–south, ahead of a tractor down the back. Time to harrow
the fallow field and plant the winter crop. Time to lay one's thinking down

in windrows. But let me fix some breakfast first; that feels like work I'm
good for. Some juice we made from some apples we picked, some eggs

the hens might have laid, if the foxes had not laid them waste first. Some ham
off the bone of a beast I wouldn't know how to raise or kill or cure. But, hey,

I know how to drop it in some virgin oil and pull it out brown and wash it
down with coffee I know how to brew on the stove. Everything, everywhere

knows what to do. And when to leave it undone. Even I, when it comes to mind
to breathe, can sometimes sit, unmade a while, and let the morning come.

Note: The poem invokes and responds antiphonally to Jane Kenyon's poem "Let Evening Come".

TODD TURNER

Camellias

The ink-printed curtain that hangs over
the window looking out onto the river,
is a silk off-white sheer number with two
mint-green long-tailed birds on a vine of
budding camellias, flowering and in bud,
seeming to pop and break in lightness
from the branch as they do in the parks
of Kyoto, Japan, or here in the town where
we live, near the library, in early winter.
We see them in the flowering months,
pink on blond wood bough, middled
with tufts of lemon-yellow anthers, but
now they're elsewhere and we are lying
in morning bliss, a rain-damp Sunday,
a rare sleep-in, restful, fingers twined,
our heads on pillows, blankets flayed
and coiled, our bodies lodged in the warm
nooks of wool and downy quilt that we
somehow in snooze make for ourselves,
touching at neck and shoulder and knee,
at ankle and shin bone, sinking in and out
of dream, of sleep, hearing the birds and
an early car, sleet tinselled on the window
where the light, in quiet movement, rises
like plumed smoke in the sheen of the
folds, as my eyes, one and then the other,
open to the bright music, to wakefulness.

Shelling Peas

Front porch, set up in a row of chairs,
given a bucket of pods, we were told to
wash the grit then prise the husk for peas.
A chore I didn't mind, I took my time
over every pail, over each repetitive task...
Snap off the ends, tear open the strip, split
the hull, pry the pod, and with a run of the
thumb, rake the peas into the pot. Repeat.

Like needle-point or roping knots, it
was work my parents were grounded in.
I hardly tired of it, just eased into a certain
order, felt a kind of rhythm at hand.
Shelling, I lulled into the routine work...
Snap off the ends, tear open the strip, split
the hull, pry the pod, and with a run of the
thumb, rake the peas into the pot. Repeat.

Soon I learnt to feel the variance between
each seam, between the notched ends,
the ridged sides. A boy, my fingers intent
and nimble as a lace maker's, I peeled
back the layers, split the husks, the green...
Snap off the ends, tear open the strip, split
the hull, pry the pod, and with a run of the
thumb, rake the peas into the pot. Repeat.

CHRISTOPHER WATSON

New Delhi

The Name deceives us.
It gives us glimpses
but nothing concrete—
unlike every building the eye can see.

The senses are on the edge, like a base jumper
on a first jump.
The scents that roll through
bring you to the brink of dry retching,
make your mouth salivate.

When the sun goes down
with the pollution lingering,
there is a apocalyptic orange glow
that overwhelms the night sky.
It lights up the street like a flare.

In the streets personal space is always in hiding.
Your ears are always on alert
to the constant blaring of artificial sounds
mixed in with the animal noises.

As I walk down the road,
I see footprints in the dust.
Like a fingerprint on a felon,
this is New Delhi's identity.

The Best Type of Sea

My feet are devoured by the cold soggy sand.
A fine depth of water hits the top of my ankles.
The grey, heavy clouds sit in the sky overlooking
the ocean that scares the fish into hiding.

I take a step into the blood-cooling liquid,
lay down my board, then let physics do its work.
In the lulls
the rounded fibreglass nose
laps the liquid glass.

My blood runs through my heart
the in a way an engine sucks in oil.
I reach the point past the seamless
swell a force that should be given respect.
When I sit up, the ocean is still, like in the eye of the storm.

The ocean mirrors the sky, showing Mother Nature's vanity.
I look towards the land.

And wait.

Editors' Notes

We offer our heartfelt thanks to David Musgrave from Puncher and Wattmann who has been instrumental in the publication of this anthology. A special thanks to the Avondale College of Higher Education creative writing class for their dedication and willingness to share their first poem-making efforts with this reading audience. We thoroughly enjoyed the writing journey with the students this semester and hope they continue to develop their craft and share creative work into the future. An enormous thank you to the established poets who have generously contributed their voices and work to this project, and have enriched so enthusiastically our collaborative vision.

The cover design for this anthology represents the professional process Donna Pinter engages in with her Avondale students from the 'That Design' studio, and we thank them all for participating in the client briefing. We acknowledge Kayla Wolf, in particular, for the skill she demonstrated in conceiving and completing the cover design. We also appreciate greatly the input on the anthology cover from Puncher and Wattmann's Matthew Holt.

We wish to acknowledge and thank Margaret House for her magnanimous contribution in assisting with the preparation of the anthology manuscript. And, for helping so happily with the *Here Not There* book launch we thank Natalie McMahon and Leticia Maguire for their unrivalled efficiency. In showcasing the anthology's launch during Learning and Teaching Week celebrations, we thank Dr Jane Fernandez (Vice-President, Learning & Teaching) for her contribution.

For their continued and unflagging support and encouragement of innovative initiatives in the School of Humanities and Creative Arts we pay particular tribute to Associate Professor Daniel Reynaud and Dr Robyn Priestley. To the many tertiary colleagues and practitioners who have passed on their good wishes for the conception and realisation of this anthology we thank them for a perennial spirit of goodwill in wanting to see poetry make its way onto the published page.

—Judith Beveridge and Carolyn Rickett
August 2012

Biographical Notes

JUDITH BEVERIDGE is the author of four award-winning books of poetry. Her most recent collection is *Storm and Honey*. She teaches creative writing at the University of Sydney, and is the poetry editor of *Meanjin*. In 2005 she was awarded the Philip Hodgins Memorial Medal for excellence in literature.

NANCY BILLIAS is Associate Professor and Chair of the Philosophy Department at the University of Saint Joseph in West Hartford, Connecticut, USA. She is currently at work on a theory of postmodern ethics, combining her interests in psychoanalytic theory, Continental philosophy, and contemporary spirituality.

KIMCHENG BOEY is a Singapore-born Australian poet. As a student he won the National University of Singapore Poetry Competition and has since received the National Arts Council's Young Artist Award (1996). He currently lectures in creative writing at the University of Newcastle in Australia. In 2006 he published *After the Fire: New and Selected Poems*, and in 2009, *Between Stations*, a book of essays.

PETER BOYLE is a Sydney poet and translator of French and Spanish poetry. He has published five collections of poetry, including most recently, *Apocrypha*, which won the Queensland Premier's Poetry Prize in 2010 and the ARTS ACT Judith Wright award. A new collection, *Towns in the Great Desert*, is forthcoming later in 2012 from Puncher and Wattmann.

JULIAN BREMNER is currently completing his final year as a Communication student at Avondale, where he attempts to balance interests in politics, writing, sports and the arts. Born in Vancouver, this ex-pat sees himself pursuing a career in foreign policy while continuing to explore the creative process, in whatever form that may take.

MICHELLE CAHILL is a poet and fiction writer from Goan-Indian background. She has published two collections of poetry, *The Accidental Cage*, and most recently, in 2011, *Vishvarupa*. In 2011 she was awarded a Hawthornden Fellowship. She is a medical practitioner and lives with her family in Sydney.

EILEEN CHONG is a Sydney poet who was born in Singapore. Her first collection, *Burning Rice* was published in 2012 as part of Australia Poetry's New Voices series. She is currently a doctoral student at the University of Western Sydney and is preparing poems for a second collection.

WILLIAM CHRISTIE, a graduate of the universities of Sydney and Oxford, is a professor in the English Department at the University of Sydney. His publications include the play for voices *Under Mulga Wood* (2004), a critical biography *Samuel Taylor Coleridge: A Literary Life* (2006), which was awarded the NSW Premier's Biennial Prize for Literary Scholarship in 2008, and *The Edinburgh Review in the Literary Culture of Romantic Britain* (2009). He is currently working on a critical biography of the nineteenth-century Scottish reviewer, editor, politician, and judge, Francis Jeffrey, with a grant from the Australian Research Council.

MTC CRONIN has written numerous collections of poetry (including several co-written with fellow-Australian poet, Peter Boyle) and a number of volumes of avant-garde cross-genre works. She currently lives, with her partner and three young daughters, on an organic farm (specialising in fresh Spanish produce) in the hinterland of Queensland's Sunshine Coast.

JOSH DYE has a fascination with obscure travel destinations, such as North Korea and Turkmenistan. He calls Melbourne home, and has a keen interest for all things sport. Josh also enjoys leadership and service, particularly combining the two overseas. An aspiring writer, he is currently studying and completing his public relations and writing internship at Avondale.

STEPHEN EDGAR has published nine books of poetry two of which have been recently published, *Eldershaw*, Black Pepper 2012, and *The Red Sea: New and Selected Poems*, Baskerville Press, Texas USA. He has also translated poems from Greek, German and Russian. He was awarded the Philip Hodgins Memorial Prize in 2006.

BROOK EMERY has published three books of poetry, *and dug my fingers in the sand*, which won the Judith Wright Calanthe Prize, *Misplaced Heart,* and *Uncommon Light.* All three were short-listed for the Kenneth Slessor Prize. A new collection, *Collusion,* is due out later in 2012. He lives in Sydney.

ERIN ENTERMANN grew up in the small agricultural town of Stanthorpe in Queensland. She recalls that her love for reading, writing and learning was ignited at a young age through frequent trips to the local library with her family. Now a second year Bachelor of Arts/Bachelor of Teaching student at Avondale, she continues to study her passions with a major in English and a minor in Music.

JANE FERNANDEZ is Vice-President (Learning & Teaching) at Avondale College of Higher Education. Her research projects include the exploration of sacralised violence, diaspora and social change, literary criticism, and the transformative value of learning and teaching. She is also interested in how social capital impacts on migrants' experiences of belonging. Jane has edited several books and is author of *The Second Skin: a Critique of Violence—The Search for Scapegoats in the Fiction of K.S. Maniam*.

JEMMA GALINDO grew up in Western Australia and has loved reading and writing since she was first introduced to books. She is currently in her first year of a Bachelor of Arts at Avondale where she is majoring in English and History. Jemma wants to work in the publishing industry, and is in the process of writing her first novel.

BROCK GOODHILL is in his final year of studying a Bachelor of Arts, specialising in Communication. He has always had a passion for writing, broadcast media and keeping up with current affairs. He aspires to follow his dream of becoming a journalist and one day hopes to enter politics.

ALTHEA HALLIDAY is a senior English teacher at Barker College in Sydney. Throughout her career she has encouraged her students to celebrate creativity and embrace the power of words. In recent times, she has discovered Dylan Thomas' *Under Milk Wood* and has taken as her mantra Thomas' exhortation to the readers of his radio play in 1953, "Love the words".

KIMBERLEY HODGKIN spent the early years of her life moving to wherever her father's job took her family. She attributes her love of travel to this and does not like to be in the same place for too long. Kimberley is a final year Communication student from Avondale, and is passionate about family and friends, health and equality in the world; things she likes to incorporate into her writing.

FERGUS HOGAN is a father with the two most beautiful sons: Lorcan (*Little Wild One*) and Caelum (*Heaven Sent*) – and he says that they are more alike than they are different: not because of him. He also says he is the "brother of two beautiful men and fathers: Darragh and Kenneth; and the first born son of Martha and Paddy". Fergus is a qualified social worker and family therapist and full-time lecturer at Waterford Institute of Technology, Ireland, where he coordinates *The Centre for Social and Family Research*. He claims to be a "wannabe poet".

CAROL JENKINS' first book of poetry, *Fishing in the Devonian*, Puncher & Wattmann, 2008, was short listed for the 2009 Anne Elder & Victorian Premier's Literary Awards. Billy Collins, the former US Poet Laureate, says "*Fishing in the Devonian* is one of the most interesting books I have had the pleasure of reading in some time. Every poem is lively with conceptual and emotional play." In 2007 she established River Road Press (www.riverroadpress.net) which produces audio CDs of Australian poetry and blogs at www.showmethetreasure.blogspot.com. Her next book is due out from Puncher &Wattmann in late 2012.

SUE JOSEPH has been a journalist for more than thirty years, working in Australia and the UK. She began working as an academic, teaching print journalism at the University of Technology, Sydney in 1997. As Senior Lecturer, she now teaches and supervises journalism and creative writing, particularly creative non-fiction writing, in both undergraduate and postgraduate programs. Her research interests are around sexuality, secrets and confession, framed by the media; HIV and women; ethics; trauma; supervision and ethics and life writing; and Australian creative non-fiction. Her third book, *Speaking Secrets*, was published this year with Alto Books.

UNIA JUMA is originally from Southern Sudan where she lived until she was ten years old. Her family then moved to Egypt and lived there for three years before immigrating to Brisbane, Australia in 2005. Now a second year student at Avondale, she is studying a Bachelor of Arts/ Bachelor of Teaching degree, majoring in Religious Studies with a minor in English.

BRIDGET KEATING is an instructor at the University of Regina and First Nations University of Canada in Saskatchewan, Canada. Her first book of poetry, *The Red Ceiling*, will be published by Hagios Press in September 2012.

JEAN KENT grew up in rural Queensland and now lives at Lake Macquarie, NSW. She has worked as an educational psychologist and TAFE counsellor, as well as teaching creative writing. Jean has published four books of poetry, her latest is *Travelling with the Wrong Phrasebooks* published in 2012, Pitt St Poetry. This has been produced as both a paperback and in a special limited edition hardback, with artwork by Sydney artist Oliver Watts.

ANDY KISSANE lives in Bardwell Park, Sydney and writes poetry and fiction. He is the 2012 Coriole National Wine Poet. His most recent collection, *Out to Lunch*, Puncher & Wattmann, 2009, was shortlisted for the NSW Premier's Prize for Poetry. A book of short stories, *The Swarm*, has just been published by Puncher and Wattmann.

RICHARD LANDER is retired and commenced writing poetry as a form of therapy after being diagnosed with prostate cancer in 2007. He is married to Lyndall and lives in Sydney. Some of Richard's other poetry has been published in *The New Leaves Poetry Anthology* and *Wording the World*.

MARTIN LANGFORD has published six books of poetry, including *The Human Project: New and Selected Poems*, Puncher and Wattmann, 2009. Thematically, he is interested in the way we try to imagine ourselves beyond our biological inheritance, and in the evolution of our social and imaginative spaces. He lives on the northern outskirts of Sydney, and the landscape of that area often features in his work. He is the editor of *Harbour City Poems: Sydney in Verse 1788-2008*, Puncher and Wattmann, 2009.

ANNE LITTLE grew up in the country Victorian town of Bairnsdale. After completing high school she decided to complete her tertiary study at Avondale and is in her last year of a Bachelor of Arts with a double major in Visual Arts and English. Learning to read late, she says she has been catching up ever since with her passion for reading and writing. Anne's other love is art, and she is currently working on a portrait she hopes to enter in the Archibald Prize.

LYNNETTE LOUNSBURY is a writer and lecturer. She teaches History and Communication at Avondale College and has written everything from short stories to documentaries. Her novel *Jack Lives Here* is out through Mad Ones Press, and she has a children's picture book due for release in 2012. She is passionate about yoga and martial arts and lives in Bronte with her partner and two wild boys.

HELENE LOW was born in Greece. She arrived in Australia at the age of two and settled in the Northern Tablelands of NSW. An accountant by profession, Helene discovered a love of poetry and creative writing later in life. She enjoys A. B. Patterson and Henry Lawson.

WIN LUBEN is a retired nurse living in Sydney who has a keen interest in learning about other cultures. Over the years she has enjoyed gardening and conversations with her Dog. She keeps her mind active with new activities like poetry writing, and some of her poems have been previously published in *The New Leaves Poetry Anthology* and *Wording the World.*

RANDY LUNDY is a member of the Barren Lands (Cree) First Nation, in northwestern Manitoba, Canada. He is the author of two books of poetry, *Under the Night Sun* (1999) and *The Gift of the Hawk* (2004), both published by Coteau Books, and he is completing a third book of poetry, *A Backyarder's Guide Toward a Vocabulary of Faith.* His poetry has been widely anthologised, including Oxford University Press' *An Anthology of Native Canadian Literature in English.* Currently, Randy resides in a village just off the Trans-Canada highway between Moose Jaw and Regina, Saskatchewan, Canada, with two Great Pyrenees and a Newfoundland dog.

CHARNELLE MACK was born and raised in Melbourne's eastern suburbs. She is currently studying a Bachelor of Arts at Avondale with a major in Psychology and a minor Communication. Her interests lie in experimenting with writing, and she aspires to someday combine her psychology degree with journalism.

BRITTANY McNITT was born twenty-two years ago in Michigan, but has planted her roots in various places around the world. Traveling to Europe, South America, and North America, she finds her writing inspiration by gallivanting through life. With camera and pen in hand, she recently arrived in Australia to study Communication at Avondale, with minors in graphic design and health sciences. She says, "There is nothing like taking a moment and making it your own, through a photograph or simply just writing it down."

BENJAMIN MILIS is a Sydneysider who has recently realised the beauty of small town life. He is currently completing a Bachelor of Arts/Bachelor of Teaching with a specialisation in Music and a minor in English. His passions lie in working at the Institute of Worship, travelling the world, reading classics and song writing by the piano.

CHELSEA MITCHELL has her heart set on experiencing every country in the world. She is a Bachelor of Arts student at Avondale studying a specialisation in Communication, and a major in International Poverty and Development Studies. She loves people's stories, and this is why she aspires to be a journalist, travel writer, novelist, and photojournalist, in the hope of giving a voice to the voiceless.

DAVID MUSGRAVE is the author of the novel *Glissando: a Melodrama.* His latest collection of poetry is *Concrete Tuesday*, Island Press, 2011. He runs the publishing company Puncher and Wattmann and lectures at the University of Newcastle.

VERA NEWSOM was born in England in 1912 and resumed writing after she retired from forty years of teaching in state and private schools. She ended her teaching career as a high school principal. In 2003 she received an Order of Australia for services to poetry. She died in July 2006. *Gratia: New and Selected Poems* was published in 2007.

JAN OWEN is an Adelaide poet who has published six books of verse, most recently *Poems 1980 – 2008.* She has worked as a librarian, editor and teacher, and has recently finished translating a selection from Baudelaire's *Les Fleurs du Mal.* She is interested in languages, travel, science, art and philosophy.

NIKARRI PARKER is a final year Bachelor of Arts/Bachelor of Teaching student at Avondale who is majoring in English with a minor in Religious Studies. She is passionate about health and fitness, literature, words and expression. Her passion for teaching stems from a desire to equip students with the tools needed to become active and engaged members of society.

DONNA PINTER lectures in graphic design and manages Avondale's student graphic design studio *That Design*. Donna also manages her own boutique graphic design studio in Newcastle—satellite ink. Poetry for Donna is often a personal creative outlet, one she has enjoyed since she was a little girl. She lives in Merewether NSW with her husband, their two beautiful girls Ruby and Coco, and their cat Claude.

CAROLYN RICKETT is a Senior Lecturer in Communication at Avondale. She is co-ordinator for *The New Leaves Creative Writing Project*, an Australasian Research Institute funded initiative for people, or carers, who have experienced or are experiencing the trauma of a life-threatening illness. Along with Australian poet Judith Beveridge, Carolyn is co-editor of *The New Leaves Poetry Anthology* and *Wording the World*. Some of favourite activities include reading and writing poetry in the company of her Cavalier King Charles Spaniel, Lily.

NOEL ROWE lived in Sydney and was Senior Lecturer in Australian Literature at the University of Sydney before his death in 2007. Before becoming an academic, Rowe was a Roman Catholic priest in the Marist Order. His books include *Perhaps, After All* (2000), *Next to Nothing* (2004) and *Touching the Hem* (2006). He assisted in the editing of the literary journal *Southerly* and, with Vivian Smith, also edited *Windchimes: Asia in Australian Poetry* (2006). In 2005 Rowe was awarded the William Baylebridge Memorial Prize for poetry, and was also invited to read his poetry at International Festivals in Rotterdam (2005) and Jerusalem (2006). He had particular interest in the interrelationship between literature, theology and ethics.

SOFÍA RUIZ is an international student at Avondale. She started her studies in Chile, but moved to Australia to finish her Journalism degree. Currently, she divides her time between studying and working part-time in Sydney.

BRUNA TAWAKE is an award winning non-fiction short story writer who has also had a love affair with poetry for the past thirty years. The poetry she writes – often for her own enjoyment – celebrates her family, her joys and her faith. She teaches public relations and event management at Avondale and manages her own public relations agency, BT Public Relations. She lives in the Central Coast of NSW with her husband, her two children and her dog.

SARA THOMPSON grew up as a third culture kid, moving frequently between Australia, New Zealand, and the USA before settling in New South Wales to attend Avondale. An avid writer since the age of five, she is currently completing a Bachelor of Arts degree specialising in Communication, and majoring in History and International Poverty and Development Studies.

She won the Signs Publishing Award for Best Original Written piece at the 2012 Manifest Creative Arts Festival, and hopes to pursue a writing career in the future.

MARK TREDINNICK has been described as "one of our great poets of place—not just of geographic place, but of the spiritual and moral landscape as well". The winner of many Australian poetry awards, including the Blake and Newcastle Prizes, Tredinnick last year took out the prestigious Montreal International Poetry Prize. His eleven works of poetry and prose include *Fire Diary* (winner of the WA Premier's Book Award), *The Blue Plateau* (shortlisted for the Prime Minister's Literary Awards, winner of the Queensland Premier's Literary Award), *The Little Red Writing Book*, and *Australia's Wild Weather*. His poems and essays are widely published in Australia and the United States. He lives on the Wingecarribee River, southwest of Sydney.

TODD TURNER is a goldsmith living in Sydney. His poems have appeared in *Meanjin, Southerly, Quadrant, Islet, Australian Poetry Journal, The Weekend Australian, Cordite* and *Overland*. He was Highly Commended in the 2011 Blake Poetry Prize and shortlisted for the 2010 Newcastle Poetry Prize. Todd is currently working on a manuscript of his first book of poems.

CHRISTOPHER WATSON lives on the Central Coast of New South Wales. He is in his third year of a Bachelor of Arts/ Bachelor of Teaching degree, majoring in History and English at Avondale. Christopher enjoys travelling and seeing different perspectives from around the world.

Acknowledgements

Judith Beveridge's poem "Japanese Cranes" is from *The Domesticity of Giraffes*, Black Lightning Press, 1987. "Herons at Dusk" is from *Storm and Honey*, Giramondo Publishing, 2009.

Peter Boyle's poem "Towns in the Great Desert (11)" was published in *Shearsman Magazine*, 83 &84, April, 2010. "Nightpoems 18/1/2012" was published in *The Stinging Fly* issue 21, Vol 2, Spring 2012.

Michelle Cahill's poem "Roses for Crianlarich" was published in *Poetry Scotland*, December 2011. "Something like a Reverie" was published in *Vishvarupa*, 5Islands Press, 2011.

Eileen Chong's poem "Five Love Poems" was published in *HEAT 25*, September 2010. "After the Wreck" was commissioned by Red Room Company in March 2012 as part of a Papercuts project for Ryan Catholic College in Townsville, QLD.

MTC Cronin's "The Manger of Words" is forthcoming in *The World Last Night*, UQP, 2012; "The Law of Necessity" is forthcoming in *The Law of Poetry*, Puncher & Wattmann, 2013.

Stephen Edgar's poem "The Sculptures by the Sea" was published in *The Weekend Australian Review*, February 18-19, 2012. "All Eyes" was published in *Meanjin* Vol 70:1, 2011.

Brook Emery's poem "After the lassitudes of blue" was published in *Snorkle #10*, October 2009. "In the hour or so" was published in *Island*.

Carol Jenkins' poem "In Loco Parentis" has not been previously published. "Silkweeds" was published in *Fishing in the Devonian*, Puncher and Wattmann, 2008.

Jean Kent's poems "In the middle of the night in the wrong part of the world" and "The Language of Light" are from *Travelling with the Wrong Phrase Books*, Pitt Street Poetry, 2012.

Andy Kissane's poem "It Begins with Darkness" was first published in *The Best Australian Poems, 2011,* edited by John Tranter, Black Inc. "Flight" was highly commended in the 2010 Place and Experience Poetry Prize and first published on the website of the School of Philosophy, University of Tasmania.

Martin Langford's poems "Greys" and "The Dragonfly" were published in *Wagtail 78*, Picaro Press, Warners Bay, NSW, 2008.

David Musgrave's poems "Ripples" and "Watermark" were published in *Concrete Tuesday*, Island Press, Woodford, NSW, 2011.

Vera Newsom's poems "Tapestry" and "Orchid Moon" were published in *Gratia: New and Selected Poems*, 5Islands Press, 2007.

Jan Owen's poems "Happiness" and "At the Persian Palace" have not been previously published.

Noel Rowe's poems "Widow of Beijing" and "On this Winter Morning" were published in *Next to Nothing*, Vagabond Press, Stray Dog Editions, 2004.

Mark Tredinnick's poem "Let Evening Come" is published on the Blake Poetry Prize website, http://www.blakeprize.com.au/news/blake-poetry-prize.

Todd Turner's poems "Shelling Peas" and "Camellias" have not been previously published.

www.ingramcontent.com/pod-product-compliance
Ingram Content Group UK Ltd.
Pitfield, Milton Keynes, MK11 3LW, UK
UKHW042008190726
13854UKWH00005B/2211

9 781921 45075